GHETTO REBELS

GHETTO REBELS

A Historical Poem

Harry Shadmon

VANTAGE PRESS
New York • Los Angeles

Published by Vantage Press, Inc.
516 West 34th Street, New York, New Yok 10001

Manufactured in the United State of America
ISBN: 0-533-08560-8

Library of Congress Catalog Card No:. 89-90181

Dedicated to the memory
Of the many who perished
And to honor the few
Who fought and survived . . .

Contents

Introduction

The play, in seven scenes, is a representation of the drama and tragedy of the rebellion in the Warsaw Ghetto. Against a background of underground conspiracy and preparation, the family of Michael, leader of the revolt, appear as the central characters. Michael himself, knowing that ultimately the revolt must fail and yet certain that it must nevertheless take place, embodies in himself the eternal dilemma of Jewry in exile. His wife, Hannah, is likewise symbolic of the mother in Israel, grave and dignified, longing for normal love and happiness, and yet conscious of inexorable forces which, generation after generation, assail Jewry and claim innocent victims.

The love of their daughter Esther for Mordecai is a love affair doomed from the start by the impending doom of the ghetto, yet both young people face the inevitable bravely, while Esther prefers death at her lover's hands to certain dishonour.

The revolt itself is vividly suggested both in detail and in broad outline—and as it mounts to its climax and then is ended in doom and the message of death pronounced by Hannah, one feels a sense of pride and defiance at the heroism of the Jews of Warsaw in those darkest days.

Prologue

On the stage illuminating the face of the reciter burns an eternal light in memory of the sacred dead of the rebellion. All else is in darkness.

Remember with reverence those heroes who chose
To challenge the Nazis and in Warsaw rose,
Who fell, but in dying sounded Freedom's bell
And brought gleams of hope to those in Hitler's Hell.

Dark days loomed for Jewry and bitter our fate,
Engulfed in mass murder and enslaved by hate.
No sure place of refuge, no balm for our fears,
No glimmer of hope to dispel flowing tears.

Yet suddenly came a new thought shining bright,
And pierced like a sunbeam the black Nazi night.
Where once one heard sobbing, one now heard the shout
Of Jewry attacking and fighting it out.

Europe accursed, drenched with Jewish blood,
Saw Jewry at bay, for they now understood,
That if there remained for them nothing but death,
At least they would fight till the very last breath.

Deep from thy soil wet with blood and with tears
Arises the cry that resounds in my ears
And borne on the wind spans the world in its flight
And calls for revolt against Hitlerist might.

What torture and anguish have thy lands not seen,
What devilish evil and terror obscene?
And mangled and torn the dead flesh testifies
Awaiting God's judgement to come from the skies.

Endless the hunger of pistols and guns
Devouring our daughters, devouring our sons,
And endless the blood that from Jewish veins welled
To redden the soil that the Nazis then held.

No end to the death camps, no end to the dead,
From Maidanek down to Savidor they spread,
To Auschwitz and Treblinka death trains would roar,
Discharging their burden, returning for more.

In mechanised tumbrils in ceaseless array
The children of Israel went their last way,
Unresisting and calm and as docile as sheep,
Our brothers and sisters went to their last sleep.

And then came the day when the hunted Jews chose
To strike back and fight—and the ghetto arose.
Eyes flashing with hatred—and arms in their hands,
The Jews stood up facing the Hitlerite bands.

Each building a stronghold, each cellar a fort
The taunts of the centuries now set at naught,
No cowardice there and no sign of dismay,
The Jew was aroused and equipped for the fray.

Revolver to tank and machine gun to plane
They hurled back the Nazis again and again,
And only when brute force and metal prevailed
Was Hitler once more as a conqueror hailed.

Yet the flame that was kindled forever will burn,
And handed to others, blaze bright in its turn,
Till Victory's garland shall reward the strife
And mankind pays homage to their Tree of Life.

No monarch has praised them or honoured their name,
No medal was issued to honour their fame,
But they need no medals and they need no praise,
These heroes of Judah shall live for always.

Renowned be forever these Jews who displayed
Great valour and vision and were not dismayed.
Who dying, yet conquered and showed to the world
The banner of Israel free and unfurled.

Dramatis Personae

MICHAEL	Leader of the rebel organisation
HANNAH	His wife
ESTHER	His daughter
MORDECAI	Fiancé of Esther
ABRAHAM	
ITZHAK	
NETKA	Staff of the Jewish Fighters'
MALKA	Organisation
SAMUEL	
JOSEF	
YAACOV	Refugee from the death camp at Treblinka
YIGAL	His son
MOSHE	Members of the Jewish
ISRAEL	Underground
LEIB	Representative of the Polish Underground

A JEWISH WORKER
FIRST GUARD
SECOND GUARD
ANDREAS   A Gestapo Officer
A GERMAN SOLDIER
A NAZI OFFICER
MEMBERS OF THE JEWISH FIGHTERS' ORGANISATION
SS MEN
MEMBERS OF THE NATIONAL COUNCIL

THE PLACE—	The ghetto in Warsaw
TIME—	Spring 1943

xv

Act I

*Ghetto melodies are heard as the curtain rises on a room in a house in
the Warsaw ghetto.* Hannah *is knitting busily;* Esther *is standing by
the window.*

Hannah
What frightens you, my child? You are so nervous.

Esther
Ah, Mother dear, I feel that evil lurks
And storm and peril are now close at hand.
So changed our lives, so poisoned seems the air,
Each corner breeding plots. How will it end?

Hannah
Be calm, my child, it is the passing guard
And nothing more; for us 'tis is nothing new,
And many weeks have passed since last they came
To seize more victims for the camps of death.

Esther
No, Mother dear, this time I have my doubts,
There seems a bitterer reason for these moves.
There in the corridor I met Mordecai,
Running upstairs and breathing heavily.
Do you remember, there were other days
How he would welcome me, his eyes alight,
His lips inspiring me with joy and hope,
Leading me forward to that magic land,
Where love and joy are deathless. But today,
He passed me running—and I wonder where.
I called out after him but all in vain,
"My heart is thine, my love, but duty calls
And to our people all my time is pledged."
So saying, in a flash he disappeared

1

Behind the door that leads to Father's room.
I chased him down the stairs, but he in turn
Eluded me and leapt toward the gate.
And now I feel I shall see him no more!

Hannah

Is this the reason for your restlessness?
You should know better than to be dismayed.
But see, your cheeks are crimson; how you blush!

Esther

[*Embracing her*]
Oh, Mother mine.

Hannah

No, Daughter, do not blush,
For such a love brings honour to your name.
The dream of love first nurtured in your soul
Discloses now its buds in beauty's flower
Proclaiming thus your longing's deep desire,
While sunbeams kiss your soul and stir your heart.

Esther

Oh, Mother, you are so good.

Hannah

But why, indeed!
For you may guess how I rejoice to see
The spring of love return in thee again.
Ah, what a joy, and for you summer's glow,
The unique summer that we know but once,
But through your happiness we can recall.

Esther

Does Father know?

Hannah

I do believe he does.
Not in concealment do your talents lie.

2

Esther

And was he angry?

Hannah

If indeed he were
Would I now turn to you and calmly speak?
"My son-in-law I shall not seek amongst
The wealthy ones," your father once declared.
"But he shall come from those whose hearts are true
Unto our cause." And Mordecai pleases him.

Esther

Oh, Mother, Mother, fortunate am I
For love indeed a wondrous thing it is
And from its very majesty I quailed.

But yet, without the blessings of you both
No calm would come to pacify the storm.
Mild has the sun to be where flowers bloom.
The dew must shine like pearls, soft breezes blow,
For where the sun beats down quite unrestrained,
There fierce winds blow and even springs run dry
So that the glory of the fields is scorched.

Hannah

Here comes your father.

Esther

Blessings on his head,
He looks quite calm.

Hannah

[Michael *enters slowly*]
Is he not always thus?

Michael

Things will be lively in the ghetto here,
But do not be afraid, cast our despair,
So long as our hearts beat, so long shall we
Seek out our vengeance for what has been.

The ravagers of Poland, Europe's scourge,
Enriched by plunder and by crime grown great,
Contrive their sordid, black and hellish plot.
This time, however, conscience is awake
And we shall not sit still with folded hands,
But from our cellars we shall strike at them
And for the rest, our trust is in the Lord.

Esther

Is it not so, Mother? I was not deceived.
Oh, awful instinct, now it has come true.

Hannah

Do you believe, Michael, that once again
The deportations will be organised?
Have they not taken from us all we have,
Freedom and wealth, what more is there to lose?

Michael

Dearer than honour and freedom there is naught,
But now our plight is more than desperate.

Hannah

Have I not earned my husband's confidence?
To know the truth, the whole truth, I demand.
Do you regard your wife as of no worth,
Who more than once has shared all risks with you?

Michael

[*Hesitating*]
No further pillage and no deportation,
But something else they plan to do this time;
No less than all the ghetto to destroy,
And ourselves with it to exterminate.
If I can trust a Christian friend of mine,
This thing is true, but till we know for sure,
For we await a special message now,
Till then I say, dismiss it from your minds.

Esther

Oh, Mother, Mother.

Hannah

Quiet now, my child,
Your father's group is strong and you must prove
A worthy daughter to so brave a man.

Michael

[*To himself while looking out of the window*]
Here comes Itzhak, and now I soon shall know
If this last outrage will indeed come true.
I see his eyes aflame with vengeful fire.

Itzhak

Only the blackest news have I brought now
The SS troops [*notices the women*] . . .

Michael

Speak loud and clear, my friend.
Will not the outcome be known to us all
For good or ill when once the foe shall strike?

Itzhak

The SS troops have been detailed, I know
To be in a position to declare
By way of birthday greetings to the Führer
That Warsaw Ghetto has quite ceased to be,
And to that end a free hand they enjoy
To burn and torture, slaughter and despoil . . .
Our communal committee lies in gaol
For having quite refused to help the scheme
By handing over the communal lists.
When the blow is to fall, I do not know,
But we will know beforehand, that I'm sure.
It is now said that they will concentrate
Their troops against us, so as to be sure.
But all in vain, for dearly shall we sell
Our lives, when they attack us in our homes.

5

Michael
Our plight is bad. Has Mordecai returned?

Itzhak
Behold, he comes.

Michael
[Esther *weeps, stays at her mother's side*]

And brings us other news,
Of our determination to resist. And you, Hannah,
I beg you to console our weeping child,
Since times are such, and bestial deeds hold sway,
Then must she learn her spirit to attune
To the dark days we live in at this time.
I have not seen her as depressed as this,
Be calm, my child.

Esther
How can I now be calm,
When even ere this happened, in my joy
My heart could find no rest, how can it now?

Hannah
Be quiet, Esther.

Esther
Look, Mother, here he comes
His brow with gloom beclouded but his eyes
Alive with flaming courage and resolve.

Mordecai
[Mordecai *enters breathing heavily*]

I come to report my duties carried out.
How great it is to take a real revenge,
Albeit small, but for my people's sake.
Westward up to the very barracks' wall
Beyond the Nazi sentries I approached

And none paid any heed to see a tramp
Or old junk dealer, which they took me for.
The refuse in my sack hung on my stick,
I passed the auxiliary police patrol,
Polluted guardians of the Warsaw Ghetto,
And likewise passed the SS guards themselves,
Who wondered not at what my sack contained
Or on what vengeful errand I was bound—
Or otherwise I would lie riddled now
A thousand bullet holes my corpse would bear.
But fortunate I was and no one stirred,
While I one endless moment had to wait,
And then counting each stride deliberately
Reached the appointed place, and far above
Heard from the barracks all the confused din.
My heart prayed for success, and swift as thought,
"The mines," I said, and joined them to the charge,
Firmly fixed to cracks within the walls.
The place where daily orders are announced
The orders to destroy and steal and slay . . .
The strands of wire I hastened to prepare;
Imagine how I felt while doing this,
Despite the nervous strain, the filth, the stench,
I saw myself in line with that old Greek
Who brought the tidings of the Marathon.
My hand was sure, I lit the match, and watched
The flame devour the strand . . . no sooner gone
To a safe distance than I heard the music,
For music was it to my eager ears,
Of the explosion scattering death around!
And then I felt, indeed, I had avenged,
In some degree, my brethren who have died.

Michael
You have, indeed, your noble task fulfilled,
And quickness, skill, and energy displayed.
God grant that you be crowned with laurel wreaths
And hailed a hero when our freedom dawns.
Your life endangered for the people's cause,

And pledged to die if need be for us all,
Your breast bared to the sacrificial knife,
In exile now yet fighting for our land.

[*He looks closely at* Mordecai]

Mordecai, I have not yet disclosed
A comrade, deeply loved, fell yesterday
Into their hands while in the very act
Of setting fire to an arms factory.
Yigal, a brother and comrade to us all
Now in the hands of these foul beasts of prey—
And then, the flames put out, was dragged away
Bleeding and broken to the prison cell.

Mordecai
Can this be true? Yigal? And now for torture
To find a way to open up his lips

[*Lifting his arms*]

Oh, Yigal, can you feel us with you now
And sharing all your torture and your pain?
Your lips will naught disclose, that well we know.
You say the Nazis put the fire out,
Then please permit me Yigal's job to do
And light the brand once more where Yigal failed.

Michael
May stars of fortune guide you on your way.
So be it.

Esther
[*Jumping up*]

No, no, it shall not be.
In God's name, please, oh, stay, my Mordecai.

Mordecai

Restrain your tears and do not mourn, Esther,
Our people's destiny is also ours,
And if the sacred front requires our lives,
Why then our future must we dedicate.

[*Aside*]

This is the fitting hour to tell him all.
Yes, Michael, your daughter I desire,
My all, my heart and soul, I worship her.

Michael

[*Placing his hands on* Mordecai's *shoulders*]

Your feelings for our daughter I have known
And though you are not blessed with worldly wealth,
Yet that is nothing in such times as these
When all that is of value is assessed
In loyalty and courage and not gold,
Weapon in hand and ice-cool brain we need.
This is the wealth we need, and this I know,
That with such wealth you are indeed endowed.
Therefore, a father's blessing on you both
And Mother, too, I know will join with me.

Hannah

Yes, youthful pair, a mother's blessing, too,
A mother's tears with heaven intercede,
And plead you may be granted peace and joy.

Michael

Not now but later shall we celebrate,
Just now the hour calls for sterner things,
For calm of mind and wisdom and resolve.

Mordecai

I thank you both and, Esther, fare thee well,
My love, I bid you also to entreat
That Heaven grant us victory this day.
Your prayers will guard me and confuse the foe
While I go forth to take a just revenge.

Esther

No, Mordecai, I see the vultures wheel
In carrion flight above thy very head,
To certain death you go, I know for sure.

Mordecai

No, Death itself dare not withstand my love.

Esther

Death will not dare! That is no balm for me.

Mordecai

Believe me, please, Death will not dare to touch
Or lay his clammy hand upon our love.
He who dares all, does all, and I am sure
The struggle brief will be, and victory full.
Come now, Itzhak. [*Waving to* Esther]
We'll meet again tonight.

Michael

One moment yet; I have something to say.
[Mordecai *and* Itzak *go out.* Esther *weeps on her mother's breast,* Michael
and Hannah *try to comfort her. When she becomes somewhat
quieter,* Michael *also goes out*]

Hannah

How are you now, my child?

Esther

A little eased.

Hannah

How you alarmed us both. Your father, too,
Who generally quiet is and calm
Was stunned to see you looking deathly pale,
Your tears so unrestrained, your grief so great.
Praise be to Go your colour has returned
And banished is the momentary pain
That cast a cloud over your youthful grace.

Esther

Oh, Mother, when he beckoned with his hand
I grew so cold and heard a warning voice.
Somewhere outside betrayal lies in wait
And in my heart I say a last good-bye.
Good-bye to love and all its eager hopes.
I feel my pulse grow weak, my heart beat slow
And near at hand I hear Death's sombre wings,
Small wonder then I could not check my tears.

Hannah

Learn to restrain your eager heart, my dear.
No easy task it is to be affianced
To such a hero in such times as these.
Great is the joy of every woman who
Can sit in gentle shade and be content
In contemplation of the bounteous fate
That filled her life with riches overflowing
And o'er her threshold many treasures brought.
Her children healthy and her man content.
For her life is a flower that unfolded,
And on all sides she tastes of happiness:
But different she, who, while life's leaves are falling

Must snatch at love and hold it while she may.
Her life is poised between distress and joy.
She sees her husband, needed by his country,
Expose his body to the bullets' flight,
Daring his all and confident of the outcome,
Sure of his cause and certain of his strength,
And loving honour no less than his life.
Honour for him, as breath for living beings:
Without it life itself not possible.
Thus, my daughter, is the man you chose,
And if you ask yourself why is your love,
You will yourself reply, "'Tis not his face,
Nor yet the gentle pleading in his voice
That draws me to him by a magic strand."
It is his spirit that you love, my dear,
His strength of purpose and his high resolve.

Esther

Be patient, Mother, with me now, I pray,
It seems, indeed, I have a lot to learn
About the inner mysteries of the heart.
Indeed at such a time a mother's care
And words of wisdom help me to endure.
Forgive me, Mother, for I must confess,
I had such visions of the days to be
And saw ourselves in the great Vale of Peace,
The Wheel of Fortune bringing us content.
How could you think that otherwise I love him
And could be satisfied to let him plunge
In headstrong rush to deepest tragedy?
I tell you, Mother, I love in him but love,
The love his singing lips declared for me,
The love that glistened in his tender eyes.
He is my love and I can love no less,
The love that murmurs like a gentle breeze
And yet can rage with fury like a storm.

Hannah

How well I do recall those self-same thoughts
When love in springtime gripped my eager soul
And swept me in its torrent to new worlds,
While the young man, afire with youthful glow
Felt in his heart the thrill of poetry.
But when the first hot ardour has been spent
And soul finds soul in deep communion,
Then will you feel yourselves most deeply bound,
With sympathies and harmonies matured,
With passions purged and earthly longings gone;
And then full majesty will love attain,
Inspiring you for all life holds in store.
The young man who on ecstasy had feasted
Now sees in life a deeper meaning still,
And where he strove with vigour unabated,
Now seeks he quietness, a port from storms.
Thus the girl, too, reacts from exultation
Since, being certain of her husband's love,
Secure and confident she now may feel.
As you are now, so was I once, my daughter,
And had we then faced times as we do now,
I, too, would have looked facts full in the face.

Esther

[*Leaning on* Hannah]
Oh, Mother, Mother.

Hannah

[*Caressing her*]
Daughter, Daughter mine.

[Michael *enters*]

Michael

A fitting sight to greet me now I find,
My wife and daughter in each other's arms
And admiration in your shining eyes.
Come then, and clasp me, too, unto your arms.
My heart is touched to see such happiness.

13

Hannah

Oh, husband dear, how many days have passed
Since I last saw you radiant as now.
Tell me, Michael, what has touched your heart
That in your eyes I read presentiments.
Has something happened?

Michael

No, wife, not yet
But I feel wonderful clasped in your arms.
And blissful visions blaze before my eyes
As if to test my very self-control.
Ah, fellow men, we must taste every fruit
And leave not one with flavour yet unknown.
Let not a moment pass untouched by joy
Nor shall there be a single arid second
When we drained not life's cup unto the dregs.
For time is short and fate impatient is,
And happiness gives none a second chance—
But instantaneous, like a lightning flash,
Has to be grasped or lost for evermore.

Esther

[*In anguished tones*]
Is there no news yet?

Michael

No, my child, not yet.
There is no need to worry yet, my dear.

Hannah

And is that all the tidings that you bring?
Do not conceal things from us, good or bad.
You know each day I dread the morrow's dawn.
Oh, Michael, you must teach me to endure
And take disastrous news with fortitude,
So that you find me worthy of the day
When for our people comes the clarion call.

14

Michael

Do not despair, nor yet give way to grief,
Not by a long way are we lost as yet
And neither helpless, for you know full well
That from some sources have we arms acquired
And if a day of terror dawns we, too,
Shall not go unresisting to our doom.
And by the way, it is as well to rest,
I'll wake you later in the day.

Hannah

Michael . . .
[*She goes out with* Esther, Michael *remains alone*]

Michael

This is the deepest crisis of my life;
All roads are blocked, there is no way to turn,
And none to save us, but our very selves.
Can any ally come to help us now?
Not even our own women know the truth,
Nor why the weapons smile their deadly smile.
Can help come from the Gentiles of this land?
That hope is weak, so what remains to do?
And Allied forces still are far away . . .
People of Israel, hated and despised,
Your children stand abandoned and alone.
But not forlorn, for from our distant land
Has come a blessing, full of hope and cheer.
"Stand fast with confidence, do not despair,
From Eretz Israel we bless you all."
[*Bitterly*]
The blessing of Our Land . . . but will they all
Receive it or break up in party strife?
Ah, Michael, all your strength will be required
To infuse courage into those too long
Accustomed not to fight but to endure.
My mind is now made up, the die is cast,
We shall rise in revolt and take revenge,
And in our action shall we light the torch

For future generations of free men.
So raise the banner of revolt on high
And sound the trumpet for the call to arms.
No sacrifice shall be too great for us,
And men and women, young and old, are braced
By faith sustained, when death has be to faced;
A faith in freedom and democracy,
And visions of their people, proud and free.

End of Scene 1

SCENE 2

Yigal is lying chained on a torn mattress, his legs thrust through the stocks. His left leg is bandaged with a torn shirt through which blood oozes. An iron door on the left, a little window with bars, opens onto a yard to the right of the stage.

Yigal

Bitter indeed it is to lie in prison
Remote from sunlight and its golden rays,
From hills and thickets filled with magic voices
Of running streams, or thunder's majesty.
But how much worse is solitude for me,
Without the comfort of my dearest friend
Who always shared my burdens and my woes,
And on whose breast I could lie down and sleep
As on a drowsy springtime afternoon
Each living creature seeks a blissful place.
Yet why should I philosophize on nature
When on all sides the prison wall I see,
Great iron doors and bars and massive bolts.
Where are you now, my brethren in distress?
Has the time come for me to say goodbye? . . .
And yet, I shall not quarrel with my fate
Nor bitter grow, nor yet deceive myself.
I dared the gallows and the prison cell,
My heart was thrilled with danger imminent.
How was it? Yes, I still can recollect,
When war began, began the slaughter, too,
And waves of frenzy swept right through the land.
The Germans made of Death a festival,
For soldiers drunk with blood and mad with rage,
With lust, and plunder as their only aims
[*From afar is heard the tune "Kol Nidrei"*]
And while they mocked at us with bloody scorn,
These pagan bullies forced the Jews to dance
Upon the very Torah for their sport,

And all this to the strains of "Kol Nidrei."
But what was worse, this beastly deed was helped
By traitors of the supplementary police,
Those thrice-accursed flatterers who bring
Disgrace upon the ghetto and themselves.
Then came the reign of terror for the Jews,
And sheer destruction was for Jewry planned.
At first cold steel achieved this fearful end,
And then came poison, at collective meals.
So fiendish the scheme, so horrible,
The victims were invited to a feast
All unsuspecting, while their gloating guards
Stood by and watched them sicken and then die . . .
This was the period of the simple ways,
Of slaying people, then came scientists
To put their talents to the basest use.
Then in their millions perished in the flames,
The Jews, with "Sh'ma, oh Israel" on their lips.
But from the ashes they will rise as victors
And testify against their murderers.
Then in the camps of death, more millions died,
By gas, the latest horrible device.
Doubtless my family, too, perished there,
[Sighs deeply and wipes away a tear]
And still we wait and still no succour comes.
Therefore, we have decided to strike back
And formed the Ghetto Fighters to redeem
Our self-respect, and our revenge to take.
For this regime no conscience holds in check.
So came I to this party and set out
To take reprisal for their bitter deeds
By blowing up a factory of arms
Where unclean Nazis made their deadly tools.
I knew at last my luck had failed to hold
And in the heat of fighting, felt a wound
That tore my leg and held me back from flight.
Good luck enough that with these flimsy rags
I managed to restrain the flow of blood
But in the wound I feel a grievous pain,

And yet this pain is very slight beside
The pain of Jewry in this tragic hour,
The suffering engendered by the deaths . . .
And yet how proudly Jewry bears itself,
Its spirit firm, unbroken its morale.
But see, someone approaches. Soon I'll know
The fate they have decided shall be mine.
[Andreas, *an SS captain, enters, armed with a whip and pistol and
accompanied by two SS men. These remain standing by the door*]

Andreas
Here is the sage, his spirit still withstands,
It seems these Jews have not surrendered yet. [*Bursting into a laugh*]
It pleases me to have defiant foes
And yet I swear to break his lofty pride.
What is your name? Where are you from? Speak up.

Yigal
A fighting ghetto Jew confronts you now
And in my faith stronger than you by far.

Andreas
Did you consider that we should degrade
Ourselves by fighting fragments such as you?
Vain superstition, when we have attained
A mighty empire, boundless as the seas,
And where our armies sit, there fear rules.
Today's events have clearly shown to us,
And your very outrage offers further proof,
That in your ghetto you have hidden arms
And provocateurs' hands are clearly seen.
Confess now who the leaders really are,
And whence your warlike stores have been obtained.

Yigal
The privilege of finding out is yours.

Andreas

You dare the Führer's spokesman to insult
And use the words of freemen—you a slave?

Yigal

[*Trying to rise*]
Perhaps you, and not I, stand here enslaved.
My hands are bound, but still my soul is free.

Andreas

Do not delude yourself by insolence
That you can turn aside your destined end.
And yet I am surprised to hear you talk;
Unusual in a race so cowardly.
Indeed this fact alone my hand restrained
Or else I would have crushed your very bones.
It pleases lions more when homage comes
Not from a cringing dog but from a bear.

Yigal

Lion, lion, I warn you that this bear
Is of your frantic roars quite unafraid.

Andreas

In my good time your secrets I'll unveil
But for the present this suffices, Jew.
I have no more to say except just this:
That if you still prefer mute insolence
And take your refuge in fallacious pride,
We have our ways to loosen up your tongue
Before you face your final, shameful end.

Yigal

In vain you strive to get me to betray
My sacred cause—but you should be warned
That all your tyranny, your cruel decrees
Are but as nothing for the ghetto Jews.
Yonder behind the ancient ghetto wall
They mock at you, experienced in death
And in our hearts we see the Wheel of Fate,
Once friendly to you, turn the other way.

20

Andreas

You stupid dreamer, can you not perceive
That fortune favours us on every side?
In Egypt are our armies firmly based,
The Bolsheviks reel back at Stalingrad,
And our New Order in all Europe rules.
The Reich supreme, all countries dominates,
While our great Führer writes new history.
Great armies scatter where our men advance
And here comes one, spared only by our kindness,
Who, in ingratitude, foretells our doom.

Yigal

This time your soldiers will be stupefied
And lose their ardour for the battle line,
On seeing that the remnant of my brethren
Knows better than your own men how to fight.
For truth and truth alone their hearts inspire,
No need to feed them on bombastic lies.
No, for they fear you not, these dauntless heroes,
As calm of purpose they draw freedom's sword.

Andreas

Yes, they are sure of death, I promise you
And tales of bravery are transient,
Which quickly fade into oblivion.
But we on victory have feasted long
In war and plunder have we had our fill,
And all the world has felt the dreaded hand,
Of Germany reborn and militant,
Of Greater Reich, immortal and supreme.
Your heroes are to certain death condemned,
As mariners who, overconfident,
Their boat against the mighty current turn,
And in a flash are foundered on the rocks
To plunge into the whirlpool's watery maze
And disappear from sight forevermore.

Yigal

You lie. For us the victory will ring
And like a star will brighten all our lives
As freedom and redemption shall be ours.
You think our visions are illusory,
And your own visions to be firm and real,
To conquer Europe, drenched in its own blood.
But this, the greatest error is of all
For we are ready to abandon all
To strike a blow for freedom's glorious cause
While Hitler's base pretensions are exposed
To mockery in days that yet will dawn.
[*As he mentions the Führer's name*, Andreas *angrily clenches his fist
and strikes the air with his whip*]

Andreas

You heard that whip crack, are you not afraid?

Yigal

The voice of free men as they stand and fight
To guard the honour of their heritage
Is stronger far than all your lashing whips.
See how your soldiers tremble at the sight
Of me defying you and unafraid.
Oh yes, accursed are you everywhere
And future generations will condemn
Your base achievements, drenched in human blood
And built on masses of our Jewish dead.
So now you know how all our fighters feel,
And none can tell you more, for that is all.

Andreas

How right you are that none will dare to tell,
And yet I have not fully questioned you.
Speak and reveal the truth, you Jewish dog!

Yigal

In vain.

Andreas

In vain, you say, but we've a way
To open up your mouth and make you talk.
[*Lashes him*]
[*He motions to one of the SS men to assist him. The lashes resound on
    the back of* Yigal. *They continue to flog* Yigal *till he loses
    consciousness. A soldier enters and hands a letter to* Andreas]

Soldier

This has just arrived for you.
[*He salutes and goes out*]

Andreas

[*Reading the letter*]
Yigal . . . his father fled. This will I use,
Perhaps great grief will cause him to relent
And for his father's honour to unbend.
[Yigal *is seen to be moving slightly*]
Are you prepared, Yigal, to tell the truth?
You see how swiftly our Gestapo works
And how exact our information is?

Yigal

[*Amazed to hear the* Nazi *knows his name, and obviously in great pain*]
I'll tell you nothing.

Andreas

Then I will tell you,
My patience with you is now at an end
And this, I warn you, is your final chance.
Your father, Jacob, still lives in our hands,
And in your hands his chance of living lies.
If you refuse to tell me what you know
I shall disclose a torture worse than death,
With agonies so terrible that Hell
In all its terrors has not equalled yet,
And in this way your father shall atone
For his son and his senseless stubbornness.

Yigal

My father Jacob? God in Heaven. Oh!
My cup of misery has overflowed.

Andreas

You see, the time has come, make up your mind
The instruments of torture are prepared.

Yigal

There's nothing left to say, that's true indeed
And there is nothing to decide, you wretch.
I am prepared for all your questioning,
[*Breathing heavily*]
Since all your words with falsehoods are infused,
Yes, you may strike and lash and torture us
And tear our bodies with your red hot tongs,
But noble fathers, noble sons deserve.
Be it in flames or be it poison gas,
Be it in street fight or the battle front,
My father will fall dead inspired by faith.
Ask him when your foul tortures reach their height,
Whether he would agree to buy his life
By treacherously giving up his son
And live exposed to national disgrace.
Yes, you may ask him then and he will shout.
With his last breath his answer will be "No."

Andreas

[*To one of the guards*]
Hans, bring in the instruments of torture
And let us see how long his lips stay sealed.
[*They close the stocks and go out*]

Yigal

What is this feeling that oppresses me
And strikes my heart and leaves it chill and numb?
It cannot be the pain in my torn leg
But something stronger, more mysterious.
How I recall July of '42
When to the ghetto's elders came the test.
Should they o'erturn the thing built by their brothers,
Or failing this, but suicide remained
Since not for them the battle underground,
Or could it be that they were unprepared?
Of course the one way they had to despise,
Which left them death as the alternative.
From me these murderers will doubtless try
To get full information of our plans
And with their torture will try to expose
The knowledge I have of the underground.
Of course no torture is too horrible,
But if the soul is strong, the flesh holds out
And will not succumb to their bestial deeds.
Already have our partisans been caught
By the Gestapo, and sometimes in fear,
Lest under torture they should craven grow
And sacred secrets to the foe betray,
They flung themselves, an action of despair,
Upon their guards, and in their death were freed.
Well done, you heroes, unknown but adored.
Therefore, Yigal, hold fast and do not flinch
If your last moments come in their fell grasp.
Though they have taken all my arms away
[Producing a razor blade from the seams of his clothes]
This razor blade will do, all I require;
How treasured is this blade to me, just now,
I knew you yet would stand me in good stead.
Let me just sharpen you a final time
So that my veins you open, swift and sure.
Quickly, I hear them coming back to me
[He cuts himself in a vein]

Only once more, my arms should not give way
When onto me these Nazis hurl themselves.
[*He takes off at the same time his bandage and blood flows also from his
leg, he falls backward*]

Andreas
[*Entering with an SS man carrying torture instruments*]

Ho, blood, what do I see, what have you done?
Faint heart, your fear must have been great indeed
At what awaited you when I returned.
We will catch you, you will not escape,
And then you'll feel the measure of our hate.
With red hot bars we will put out your eyes,
And time and time again you shall endure
Appalling tortures till we make you speak.
[*A hand holding a revolver comes through the window, four shots are
heard,* Andreas *and his assistant fall to the ground*]
Hell . . . [Andreas *dies*]
[*The SS man with his remaining strength fires at the attacker, but only
laughter is heard, dying away in the distance*]

Yigal
[*Recovers consciousness for the last time*]
Blessed art thou, my brother in this strife,
Although you came too late to save my life,
At least I know that you have made them pay
And taken full revenge on them this day.
My death is near, but even as I go,
I feel my people's triumph o'er the foe.

End of Act I

26

Act II

SCENE 1

Esther *is waiting in the conference room of the leaders of the Jewish Fighters' Organisation. At the side a wide window opening onto the ghetto centre.*

Esther
Full half an hour have I my love awaited
And darkness fell more than hour ago.
Has he forgotten that I am tormented
And shall not rest until I hear his voice?
Soon will the meeting start, then I must leave.
Yet how he left me, confident and strong
Although Death's talons seemed him to await.
Has he succeeded to evade those horrors?
[*She looks all around the room*]
This place instills in me a deadly trembling
As if some fearful secret lay entombed.
Ah well, here broods the spirit of resistance
And these four walls for vengeance cry out.
Listen, I hear a footstep in the passage.
Who can it be? Whose step is it I hear?
It is my love? Oh, Mordecai, welcome.
So late for you to come to your betrothed.
[*Runs toward him and hugs him*]

Mordecai
How wonderful. We are alone together
And now I can disclose to you, my dear,
How much it means to be in your embrace,
How fortified I feel when you are near.

Esther
Do I indeed inspire you, my darling?

27

Mordecai
What else, if not the love I bear for you?
[*He presses her to his heart*]
Esther, hear of our most recent triumph.
I reached the factory with my companions,
But Nazi groups kept guard along the route
And I perforce had to dismiss my men.
Then I alone approached the prison cell
Where I shot down the foul Gestapo captain,
The black and criminal Andreas himself,
The while he stood and glowered over Yigal,
Who lay before him, bleeding from his wounds.
You may imagine how I felt just then,
And as I struck him down I knew full well
That we are fighting for our own existence
And from this bitterness new hope will rise.
We have reached unity these darkest days
And found each other in the test of strife.
Great are the prizes we are pledged to win.
The storms may rage about us, but we know
That we have forged a weapon for the fight
That will withstand whatever tests may come.

Esther
All this, Mordecai, I, too, have felt most strongly
Blowing about me like a raging wind
And chilling me unto my very heart,
Until I feel the pangs of fiercest fear.
When this revolt breaks out into the open . . .
It haunts my merriest moments with its thread.
And then my father gave me his last blessing,
How hurriedly he gave it—then was gone,
To be immersed within my people's fight.

Mordecai
Do not be angry if I speak my mind,
Nor think me disrespectful if I say
That such a blessing have I always craved.
It seems to me that women always seek

Too detailed an assurance of their fate,
And hanker after quietness and peace.
We men in truth a different faith have earned,
That strikes like lightning with no warning note
At such a time when hearts are beating fast,
When sword in hand we face that Nazi foe,
At such a time his blessing have I sought.
And yet, all is reversed, but matters not.

Esther

Do not be vicious.

Mordecai

Do not call me that.
In love I am and also keen to strike
A blow to help our people in its fight
And if death comes—in that shall be my pride.

Esther

How can you be so cruel, to speak of death?
Can you forget our love that doth lament
Our constant partings and our bitter fate?
And now I lose you, too. Oh, who can judge
The misery that overwhelms me now?

Mordecai

Not without you have I desired to die,
But if it had to be, then in my arms.
What else has this world now to offer us
Save useless wealth that we do not covet?
Only in achievement am I now inspired,
In that alone we must remain content,
And as for worldly things, we must wait.
Perhaps the next world will vouchsafe us them,
And if there is one thing I still regret
It is the passions' secrets have remained
Forever closed and secret still to me.
Here every moment fortune takes new turns,
But there my fortune is unchangeable.

Esther

Take me with you in some enchanted boat
And we shall ever journey on together,
But let us not too soon forsake the earth
Which draws me, be its misery so great,
The earth for me is still a pleasant place
Despite the many evils that exist.
Nurtured on hope sweet blossoms yet arise
And grow in tribute to a constant faith.
Yes, Mordecai, I find life very sweet,
And sweeter since the day I loved you first,
For on that day I felt the surge of spring
And in my heart the world awoke with joy.
Yes, on that day I knew that life was sweet
And felt alive and vibrant and inspired.

Mordecai

Esther, my dearest, my betrothed love.

[*They embrace*]
Esther

If only I could always feel you near.

Mordecai

I hear the voices of my friends draw near,
They come to meet your father, I must go.
May all be well with you, beloved one.
Another kiss—may peace be with you now.

Esther

Do not destroy my loving dream so soon.

Mordecai

Would that I could, my conscience torments me now.
So live in peace, my darling, live in peace.
[*Goes out*]

Esther

Live in peace! Wherefore am I forsaken?
My heart is filled with grief to see his tears.
The atmosphere around him seems so gay
As if to promise him that all is well.
Can it be true that all this joy is spent
And that the sun will shine on us no more?
With him beside me I can feel triumphant,
But all alone I am o'erwhelmed with grief.
Where has he gone, light of my very life?
He is so pure, the fount of all my love.
But now I am submerged with bitter dreams
And seem to see the ghetto wreathed in flames.
Would I had stifled this my love for him
And quenched my ardour ere it came to this.
[*Goes out*]
The leaders of the underground enter. There are six men and two women.
   Netka, Malka, Michael, Abraham, Mordecai, Itzhak, Samuel,
   and Joseph. *They take seats in a half-circle around* Michael.

Michael

This fateful hour now sees us here assembled
On our decision all Warsaw Jews await.
Our spokesmen by Gestapo have been seized,
And with them the communal leaders, too,
For failing to provide a list of names
Of all the Jews who still remain alive.
This is the fiendish plan of Hitlerism,
To keep alive none but the Jews who slave
To make the armaments that Hitler needs.
These and the special police and traitor guards
Are to be spared because they are of use.
The rest—would find new work far in the woods.
But though they had the promise of the Germans
That none would harm them if they would agree,
Yet all refused, mindful of past experience.
Steinfort, the Nazi commissar, it was
Who hoped thus to deceive them, but was foiled
In his attempt to strike two blows at once,

31

And in so doing, perhaps enrich himself.
Therefore, he said, to show how kind he was
That this time he would not be obstinate
And if they only raised a certain sum,
A giant sum indeed, he would forgive.
So now they wander through the wretched streets
And seek this ransom that he has imposed.
There is no need to tell you what I think;
I want to hear the viewpoints of you all.

Itzhak

Your point of view is known to us indeed,
And as for me, I have but one desire—
To face our tyrants openly and soon.

Mordecai

For such an aim, I trust, are we assembled.
Why else would we have trained an eager youth
If not to fit them for the battle line?

Netka

I, too, am of your mind but also feel
That not alone should we rise in revolt.
We should contact the gentile partisans
And with their aid prepare to strike the blow.

Samuel

Our movement is as yet some thousands strong
But tens of thousands in this ghetto live.
Would you so have it that they turn aside?

Mordecai

It could not be that they would stand aside;
I know that with us they will dare the storm.

Joseph

I have one fear that haunts me endlessly.
Can we be sure that none will us betray?

Malka

If there are traitors, we shall root them out
And mercilessly clear them from our ranks.

Itzhak

Those who with odious flattery serve our foes
Shall share the fate of Nazi beasts themselves.
And as for traitors, we shall let them see
That as the Nazis die, so shall they, too.

Michael

Now, Abraham, what is your point of view?

Abraham

As some great earthquake surging in our midst
Arises hope within the ghetto walls
I seem to see a mighty space unfold.
[*Points to the window*]
Before it stands a gate through which must pass
The multitudes that walk the way of death.
Upon the gate in letters large inscribed
A dreaded text: TYPHUS AND LEPROSY.
When this appeared less than three years ago
We numbered more than half a million strong.
And now how many live to tell the tale?
Not more than forty thousand have survived.

Mordecai

It is not quantity that will decide,
One stone thrown in the sea can bring to life
A million ripples from the ocean bed.

Abraham

I know myself that what you say is true
And merely raised the matter to recall,
To all of us, the horrors we have seen,
When every corner hid a deadly threat,

And our brethren trembled for their lives,
Lest they were snatched away for having dared
To walk about without the yellow star,
While little children wandering in the town
To beg a crust of bread from passersby
Were shot like criminals and done to death.
Likewise a bullet in the back befell
A butcher who had sent a little meat.
Death for attending prayers in synagogue,
Death for selling cloth, or even books,
Death for speaking during hours of work,
Death for attempting to sew up a shoe,
And death for helping to alleviate
The victims of the epidemic waves.
Day and night death menaced, all the time
During those long and monstrous, weary years.
Who has not heard the riddled bodies fall?
Who has not had his nightly hours spoiled
By Nazis searching out of pure sadism?
Who has not seen the long lines of slave workers
March off at dawn to serve their Nazi masters,
Who roared out all the while their ribald songs,
"When Jewish blood beneath the knife shall spurt."
How good it is to contemplate revenge.
Day after day their victims still march out
Their bodies from starvation all malformed
And clothed in rags, and filled with nameless fear.
But now we shall avenge them and fight back.
We know that we cannot restore to life
Those broken victims who lie in the grave.
On whom the murderers rehearsed their art
And practised their appalling butchery.
This Warsaw Ghetto is a prison vast
Founded on horrors, based on misery.
And now one question waits for our reply,
Can we rely on the Gestapo's word?
The answer is too plain to all of us.
Our ransom will into their pockets go
And once paid, that will not be the end.

Each time for money will the tyrants ask
So long as anyone remains alive.
My mind is made up, and it is as yours;
The hour for retribution surely strikes.
This is the hour for which we all have yearned—
Strike while the iron still is hot, I say.

Michael

I see that most of us are of one mind.
All that remains is where to rouse the mass,
Since I am sure that Mordecai is right
In saying that they all will follow us.
We will I know also receive consent
From members of the National Committee
Although they may to caution be inclined
And fail to see how urgent is the hour.
Whereas for us the fateful hour has struck
And in death's shadow we must fight for life.
Our flag in self-defence has first unfurled
In days gone by, but not against the foe,
For plague and hunger were our enemies,
Yet we held on, abstaining from attack,
Believing that the Allies would succeed
And win for us, while we endured and hoped.
In those same days we suffered from within
From traitors and informers who would pledge
Their very soul to earn a moment's grace,
And with foul tongues their lying rumours spread
To poison hopes and sow seeds of discord.
Yet it is true, we had our share of these,
But other nations have their Quislings, too.
And when time's wheel revolves through its full course,
These traitors will receive their just deserts.
Netka, you know the orders for your troop,
Ere midnight strikes they must eliminate
All German agents festering in our midst.

Netka

With joyful hearts and conscience white as snow
We shall destroy all our fifth columnists,
And cut off at its source the treachery
That helped the Nazis to impose their rule.
Once this is done, they shall not easily
Find victims for their murderous designs.

Joseph

Forgive me if I raise another point.
Our weapons. Do you think they are enough
To give us victory once fighting starts?

Michael

Not only that, but we have profited
From our experience last January,
When first we organised to test our strength.
The SS men and the militia Guard
Swept through the streets like beasts in search of prey,
But in their paths stood some of our own men,
Who held their ground and stopped the Nazi tide.
Do you remember how they were surprised,
When on their heads a shower of stones rained down,
From nearby windows and from every roof?
Nor did it help the Nazis when they leaped,
Revolvers drawn, onto the balconies,
For there our girls stood guard, with vitriol
With which they blinded all who ventured near,
Until our parties had been reinforced
And drove the Germans off in headlong flight.

Joseph

Yes, but a heavy price was paid for that,
And from the hostages the Germans slew
More than a hundred as a grim revenge.

Mordecai

Where is the war that is not paid in blood?
We cannot change the manners of the world.

And from that day we gained a long respite
As though our enemies had been convinced
That we had ceased to be a helpless prey.

Michael

We have indeed passed through some fearsome days
Since when we first our movement organised.
And nothing but a foolish dream it seemed.
Do you remember Joseph when we had
Our first revolver—and did not despair
Until today we look on what has been
And see how we have triumphed over odds.
When races fight for their survival, then
No weapon is too trivial or too small.

Joseph

I do not disagree and yet still think
That we should make an effort to obtain
More weapons from the Polish partisans
And from the Allies, if it can be done.

Netka

Did we wait for Russia to appear
And prove our saviours, but where are they?

Michael

Vain hopes, my brethren, they are distant still
But though they have the German foe repelled,
Not them alone can we now criticise.
Do you remember how we used to hope
To rouse the world's opinion to our side,
As when we sent a cryptic telegram
Informing them that "Mr. Amos stood
By what he said upon the third of May"?
That is to say, for all who understood,
That if the book of Amos they inspect
In chapter five, verse three, they will perceive
The prophet's words to be, "The city where
A thousand live, a hundred shall survive,

And where a hundred live, shall live but ten
To carry on the torch for Israel"
[*In great bitterness*]
You all remember what the answer was . . .
Nothing at all, in our great hour of need.
Our pleas to the democracies were vain
For not with protests can the foe be stayed,
But rather must be met on his own ground
And fought back with the weapons of his choice.
No politics can help us in our plight,
And threats of retribution serve no end.
Slaughter and torture have persisted still
More terrible than anything endured
Since mediaeval times with blood were drenched.
No one believes the truth of what we wrote,
And when they will believe, it will be late,
For they will tread on corpses piled in heaps
Or see great piles of dust that once were men.
Then will their conscience smite them but in vain,
And in the meantime we are left alone,
And yet the valiant strongest is alone . . .
[*Three double knocks are heard on the door.* Moshe *enters. He is one of
the house guards*]

Moshe
Forgive me if I interfere like this
But to my mind it is a matter grave.
A workman who has managed to escape
Has something urgent to disclose to you.

Michael
Let him come in and tell us what he knows.
[Moshe *calls the worker who comes in, tired and dressed in ragged clothes*]

Workman
Shalom to all of you. I bring you news
Of new calamities for us prepared.
Today, as every day, to work we marched

Suspecting nothing, till we found ourselves
Lined up in the new cemetery
And told to dig mass graves, and as we stood
We saw a line of women captives come
And ordered to stand by the open graves.
While grinning Nazis said, "Be patient please,
Your husbands soon will come to join you here."
With three more workers I made my escape
And through back streets and subterranean ways
I reached you here as soon as possible.
The ransom that we paid was but a trick
And our own graves already are prepared.

Michael
We are indeed indebted to you, friend.
It is as well that we should be prepared
To face whatever dangers are in store.

Workman
Whatever you command, we shall obey.
[*Goes out*]

Michael
Have you still doubts, Joseph, or have you seen
That the community awaits our lead?

Joseph
I have no further doubts about it all.

Michael
Now we must act, there is no time to lose,
And each to his allotted task must go.
Abraham, contact the committee men,
And Malka, you must arrange to see
The leader of the Catholic partisans.
And you, Netka, on you we all rely
That not a traitor shall tomorrow see.
At midnight we shall gather here again.
Downstairs, in the cellar, shall we fling

39

Our gauntlet in the face of Destiny
And final details of the rising plan,
In preparation for our vengeance.

Abraham
Till midnight then.

Malka
We must indeed work fast.

Netka
Traitors shall know that justice still exists.

[*She goes out with the others.* Michael *is left alone; he goes to the window and looks at the roof*]

Michael
Here is my tortured city, tense and torn
And yet one dreams of peace to come one day.
Peace . . . the very word seems far away
To citizens who see the silent streets
Once filled with life, where now nobody stirs.
My Jewish brothers in their beds, dream not
That ere another dawn revolt will strike
And that they will be called to play their part.

[Hannah *has meanwhile come in through the near door, and from the side approaches* Michael. *She hears his final words*]

Hannah
The die is cast then, Michael, is it not?

Michael
There is no other way; we must revolt.

Hannah

Fate has committed to you, in your care,
Thousands of souls, and yet you seem to think
That with you lies the right, as you may wish,
To send them to their doom in this revolt.
How can you do this, and risk others' lives?
You could indeed have risked your own, of course,
Or even those about you, in your home,
For we have pledged ourselves unto the death.
But all these others, who gives you the right
To tempt the Angel of Death with their souls
And put an end to things that are not yours?

Michael

Better thus than die helplessly
At Nazi hands, as we have done before.
And also, think not that we all are doomed,
Our strength perhaps is greater than you think.
Why do I feel so sad? Whence come these tears?
The people's need our hearts must dominate
And all our private feelings must await.
[Hannah *leans her head on his shoulder and weeps bitterly. The curtain falls quickly*]

End of Scene 1

41

SCENE 2

In the cellar the leaders of the ghetto are meeting. The leaders of the Jewish Fighters' Organisation and members of the council are engaged in a fierce debate. With them is sitting the representative of the Polish Underground.

Michael

Silence. This way we never can agree
And time is passing in sterile debate.
Are you not ashamed so foolishly to act
In front of one from Poland's underground?
Do you not realise that fate has called
And that no other way exists for us?

Leib

The National Council holds another view
And we are sure your plan has fatal flaws.
Must we throw down the challenge of brute force?
Perhaps they will leave us in peace just now,
And if so, why tempt fate with mad revolt?

Mordecai

This is the most exasperating view.
When will these people realise the truth,
That we have changed and can meet force with force?

Abraham

Besides, the sons of Poland will not fail
To send us help. What can you say for them?

Jan

As representative of Poland's underground
I am empowered to promise you our help,
And all the parties in our movement join
With me in wishing you a victory.
Our differences with Poland's government
That sits in London, still exist you know,

But our joint hatred is a binding link
And insofar as liberation calls,
All men are brothers who true freedom seek.
You may be sure that we will help you now.

Michael
Well, brothers, are you still oppressed by doubts?
What is the hurry to revolt, you ask?
Let him give answer, who can tell you all.
[*Looks at his wristwatch*]
Each moment now, Yaacov, he should be here,
A man of Warsaw, from the camp of death,
From Treblinka, by God's grace escaped.
Learn from his lips the horrors that take place
And what awaits us at the German's hands.
[*He turns towards the side entrance, and steps are heard. Yaacov enters
      with two guards*]

First Guard
This is the place; here is the ghetto council.

Mordecai
Whom do I see? The father of Yigal.

[*To* Michael]   **Second Guard**
The orders to us have been carried out.
[*The guards go out*]

Yaacov
Where am I now? I cannot still believe
That after endless days and nights in flight
I find myself with friends and not with foes.
My brother Jews, my brothers in distress.
[*Turns to* Mordecai]
Ah, you, my friend, I seem to know your face.
Were you not one of my son Yigal's friends?

Yes, yes, you are Mordecai, where is my son?
Does he still live?
[*All eyes are on* Mordecai, *who shakes his head and wipes away the tears from his eyes*]
Why are you silent now?
My eldest son, pride of my very heart,
How did he die? Was it in German hands,
Or did he lose all hope and kill himself?

Mordecai

He died the death of heroes, brave and true,
A worthy son and warrior for truth.
He died in German hands, but is avenged.
His murderer by our own men was slain,
And it may be that knowing this, you will
Feel comforted a little for his sake.

Yaacov

Feel comforted? After what I have seen?
I can feel nothing, neither love nor hate.
And have been purged of all that life holds dear.
A miracle of God it was, no less,
That we escaped out of the camp.
Doubtless you wonder how it came to pass
That from the very deathhouse I broke loose;
A sorry tale indeed I have to tell.
We had been chosen as skilled labourers,
And with some other scores from Warsaw, too,
Were allocated heavy manual work
As navvies, builders, yes, and scavengers,
And then the most appalling job of all,
To bury our own dead, the murdered Jews.
And though we felt the pains of deep fatigue
Far worse than this, we felt our aching hearts
And we have seen it all, how old and young
Have faced their ghastly doom at Nazi hands.
Then when extermination was decreed
The camps were sealed off from the outside world
And only Nazis could come in and out.

But crimes like this will not remain concealed
And from the earth's four corners will resound
A cry for vengeance and blood for blood.
Until the day of vengeance comes indeed
When our oppressors, haunted in their dreams,
Shall plead in supplication, but in vain.

Malka
Would you not like to rest before you tell
Of these foul horrors that disturb your mind?

Yaacov
No, no, I know not how long I may live,
So listen to me while I still can speak.
Well are they named the death trains; those that go
With their dread cargoes to the final camps.
Ah, what a horror greeted us therein,
A multitude of corpses, piled in heaps,
Naked and mangled, scattered on the ground,
Their faces swollen and gas-blackened still,
Their eyes still staring sightlessly in space.
But day by day the heaps of corpses change
And endlessly new victims are hurled in
To feed the endless hunger of the beast.
Infants are snatched from mothers, men from wives,
And so it went on, death, and blood and tears . . .

Michael
Accursed brutes, for all this they shall pay;
We shall revenge our brethren to the full.

Yaacov
Hopes rose and fall but no relief appeared . . .
The flower of our race passed through their hands
Young girls, their bodies cruelly defiled,
Ravaged as virgins then to death consigned,
And as for us, if we so much as paused,

45

A bullet in the head was our reward.
As for our guards, to them it was a sport,
As when a mother, child clutched to her breast,
Frantic with terror, fled toward the gate,
Although she had no hope to get away,
And yet the guards, imbued with sadism,
With leaden hail from their machine gun post
Slew both of them, and laughed aloud in joy . . .
We also had some doctors in the camp;
That is, as such they did describe themselves,
Although their acts told quite a different tale,
For far from curing any sicknesses
They sought to stimulate them by new means,
And with injections into victims' veins,
They rotted bodies with bacteria.
At other times, they tried out deadly gas
And not a day passed without some new proof
Of German savagery and lust for blood.
Sometimes, when hanging was the victims' end
The Germans pulled the nooses gradually
So that the final moments would be drawn
And agony prolonged before the end.
Oh God, the first time I beheld all this,
I stormed and raged and tore my very hair;
The shrieks of children and the cries of pain
Still haunt my dreams and torture all my hours.
Then came the baths, a new and fiendish trick.
Before the journey all the Jews were told
That they must take a shower, so they undressed.
For safekeeping, they said, all valuables
Were taken by the guards, "just for a while"
And through the megaphones loud voices bawled
That they must hurry ere the water cooled.
But once inside, no bath awaited them,
Rather did death itself beckon them on.
Some carried children, cherishing the hope
That thus the horrid gas they would avert.
Others would break away in futile flight,
But dogs urged on by guards would hurl them down,

46

Then came the dreaded moment; doors would close,
Wild shrieks and groans—then silence would ensue.
Each twenty minutes a new cargo came
And when the doors would open, crushed inside,
The dead still stood, together as in life,
Perhaps indeed the easiest way to die.
Devoid of all emotion, mere cold flesh,
No love or hate or ugliness or charm,
No jealousy, or poverty, or wealth.
So each succeeding day the numbers rose
And sometimes we would recognize the dead
As members of our families, or friends,
But no words came, our lips were paralysed . . .

Jan

Is it a fact that the Ukrainians
Were foremost in the looting and the crime?

Yaacov

They plundered, robbed, like all our other guards,
And many even went to extreme lengths
To curry favour with their Nazi chiefs.
Nothing was left, and even dentists came
To rob the dead of silver and of gold,
While others sought for jewels and for rings
And even cut off fingers or whole limbs
When otherwise they could not get them off.
Then at long last came our own fearful task;
To drag the corpses into giant graves.
You will not be surprised if I disclose
That from amongst us many took their lives
Unable to continue with the work.

Michael

During those months, did none dream of revenge,
Nor seek a means of showing resistance
And selling their lives dearly while they could?

47

Yaacov

Yes, there were incidents much as you say
And one of them I never shall forget.
It was the time when girls were being picked
To gratify the Germans in their lusts.
Among them one, so beautiful and young
That symbol of Jewish womanhood
She might have been, in better days than ours.
In her the spirit of resistance burned,
And with a gun snatched from a guard nearby
She shot two Germans and then stood at bay.
Naked she stood, majestic in her pride
Then turned and dashed toward the wire fence.
But as she climbed it, from the control room
The Nazis switched the electric current on,
And she fell back, another sacrifice.

Netka

She is for us the symbol of our fight.

Malka

Her deed shall like a beacon for us shine
And light the way in the dark days ahead.

Abraham

This was an act of bravery by one,
But did not it inspire the multitude?

Yaacov

Once only was resistance organised.
We in our huts already lay asleep
When shouts and shots disturbed the silent night.
Then quiet once again . . . and in the dawn
We saw the courtyard filled with recent dead,
Who had refused to meet their doom like sheep
And snatching up whatever came to hand
They sold their lives, but dearly, and now lay
Cold and stiff but scornful of their foes.

Itzhak
Did they not make the effort to escape
From that black Hell that threatened them always?

Yaacov
In vain such idle hope, when doom awaits.
The fates decided and the victims died.
Those who escaped were caught and hung at once.
I see him yet, my Warsaw friend, Michael,
And from the very gallows he proclaimed
"Long live the Jews, and death to Hitler."
No sooner spoken, than his soul had fled.
One day came Himmler, archfiend of them all,
Accursed be his name forevermore.
He gave the order to burn all the dead
Lest one day evidence should come to light
From Poland's sacred ground and be the cause
Of bringing them to justice for their crimes.
A fearful stench arose from each great grave.
Day and night machines dug up the dead,
And crumbling corpses, piled in mighty heaps
Were drenched in petrol and then set on fire.
Such scenes as this one dare not recollect,
To see one's brethren vanishing in flame.
Sometimes a pregnant woman would be hurled
Onto the flames, and give birth to the child
So that it lived and died as in a flash,
No sooner born than eaten by the fire.
At times they threw the children in first
And then mocked the mothers who were made to stand
To see their infants murdered, by their cries
Of "If you really love them, save them now,"
So that these mothers, goaded to despair
Dashed in the flames and perished with their young.
Dust is all that remains of millions,
Dust that has settled within Poland's soil
And doubtless will enrich the Polish earth,
That if it could, would tell a sombre tale
Of martyrdom and murder without end.

But earth is tongueless so for us the task
To speak and testify of what has been.
So day succeeded day and all the while
We toiled and toiled to cover up the dust
With cleaner earth, and so remove all trace
Of all the crimes committed in that place.
Often, among the mangled limbs and bones
One saw a finger pointing to the sky
In accusation of its murderers
And calling on the world to take revenge.
At such a sight, even the hangman paused
While we beheld it as a sign from God.
Oh, may it be that our design succeeds.
How long ago it seems when first we dreamed
Of striking back, not dying passively.
And now the challenge has been given us,
Each man must do his duty to the full.
But let me tell you how we broke away.
You know Ukranian guards are easy prey
To any chance of robbery or loot,
And while they were diverted in this way
We snatched up a machine gun from their hands
And fought our way toward the armoury
Then with one burst of fire we blew it up.
A giant tongue of flames leapt round the camp
And seared the buildings with its mighty blast
While we, triumphant for one fleeting spell
Broke through the gate and made good our escape,
And in the forest breathed once more free air
And rendered thanks to God for his great help.
Not easily, however, are those scenes
That were enacted daily in the camps
Obliterated from one's memory.

[*A shadow picture appears on the wall. A baby impaled on a bayonet,
    bleeding. Then a second shadow picture. Two hands rending a baby
    in two. A mother's shriek is heard, and from afar, weeping*]

Do you not see the visions that return,
Can you not hear the awful shrieks of pain?
Here a monster rends a living babe
And dashes out its brains against a wall.
There hangs Michael, dearest of my friends,
[*A voice is heard calling "Long live the Jews. Death to Hitler"*]
From the gallows prophesying doom.
And there the hand, can you not see the hand
In fiery letters, not for Nazi eyes,
[*A giant hand appears on the wall, the index finger stretched out and
     writing*]
"Mene Tekel Ufarsin," it writes,
The words, which for Belzhazzar spelt his doom.
[Yaacov *steps toward the shadow and falls unconscious*]

Mordecai
Come quickly, help, lest he die at our feet.
[*Trying with the others to help him up*]

Malka
Sacred old man, is it a sleep or death?
See, he stirs; his eyes are opening.

[*In delirium*]   ### Yaacov
My brothers, is it not Passover Eve,
Let all the needy come and celebrate
The great redemption of my people see:
This coming year shall see us proud and free.
[*He dies*]

Michael
May his soul with the Infinite be bound;
His sacred memory shines like a torch.
Your words for us were crowning evidence
In accusation of the murderers.
[*To* Leib]
And do you still retain your former view
And wonder if we really need revolt?

51

Leib

No, no, as certain as the very sun
There is no other path for us to choose.
Our strength a raging torrent shall become
And all the ghetto join us in the fight.
For now no one can fail to understand
That death or freedom is our battlecry.
Therefore, we fight. There is no other way.

[*With great emotion*]   ## Michael

Come now, my brethren, since we are agreed.
This modern Amalek stands over us
And threatens with destruction all the world.
Therefore, let us like other nations rise
And in revolt our independence seek.
Rebellion has been smouldering in our hearts,
But now the glowing embers burst in flame.
Pass on my orders to your sections now
To all our members in the ghetto bounds
We shall redeem the honour of our race
And fight for truth and liberty and life.
This time we are united and resolved
And no more party differences exist.
From intellectuals to the working class.
From Zionists to Marxists—all are one,
This is no time to think of death or fear,
We know that if our destiny is death
That we shall bravely die, our heads held high.
Yes, we love life indeed and would have sought
To sample all life's joys, in better days,
But since the Nazis decreed otherwise
We shall not flinch or draw back from the task.
Pay no attention to the multitudes
That shall be massed against us by our foes,
Since one firm heart can stand against a storm
And in my heart I feel the added strength
Of all the Jews scattered throughout the world

And filling us with mystic confidence.
As they have confidence in us, so we
Must in ourselves feel sure of victory.
Go proudly to the fight, and if I fall,
Before my earthly span runs its full course,
Then Abraham, comrade-in-arms of mine
Shall take my place to lead you in the fight.
This is my order; spread it far and wide;
Whoever leaves his post, stands self-condemned;
Whoever with the foe communicates,
Whoever in his action and his speech
Reveals himself a danger to us all,
That one shall die, at once and on the spot,
For as we stand, we cannot tolerate
The slightest injury unto the cause.
And those who doubted us, shall know tonight,
When all known traitors are disposed of.
As for the Nazis, take no prisoners.
We have no food to waste upon those dogs,
And quarter shall we neither give nor ask.
Those who have so long spilt our Jewish blood
Shall now themselves, be slaughtered at our hands
And pay the penalty for all their crimes.
Remember how, he who a lion slew
And drove before him hosts of Philistines,
Even great Gaza's gate aloft he bore.
Then captured and a plaything for his foes
Did Samson pull the temple pillars down,
And in his death, victorious emerged,
Triumphant at the moment of his end.
Take heart from this, that what may seem defeat
Is really victory in other guise
[*Raises his right hand*]
Therefore, I swear a solemn oath today
And call on God to hearken to my words
To fight unto the end and not forsake
My brethren of the ghetto, at my side,
And to strive on till victory is ours,

Or death brings its oblivion and its calm.
Swear it with me, comrades from the ghetto.
[*They all lift their right hands*]

Abraham and Mordecai
We swear our people's honour to defend
And to this rising our lives dedicate,
Till death itself, while blood flows in our veins.
Till death itself, while blood flows in our veins.

Netka and Malka
We swear our victims have not died in vain,
"Long live revenge," our battlecry remains
Till death itself, while blood flows in our veins.

Martial music accompanies the end of
Act II

Act III

SCENE 1

In the trenches. Moshe *and members of the Israel Fighters' Organisation and dragging a heavy sack to a hiding place.*

Moshe
Here, if you need it, is another proof
That even priests have risked their lives for us
To keep us well supplied with warlike needs.
But they themselves are harried and pursued
And after this no more we shall receive.
It seems as though no further food will come
To feed the workers in the ghetto walls.
Potatoes, look, but what is there beside?

Israel
A pistol and these hand grenades, you see.
Four tommy guns and sticks of dynamite.
How much I hated weapons long ago,
As things for murder fitted, and naught else.
But how things change, and on this very day
I wish my body were with arms encased.

Moshe
If only they all knew just how to use
These weapons; then lots of time would we have saved.
[*They hide the sack*]

Israel
It would have well repaid us, had we toiled
Through day and night to forge more deadly steel,
The steel with which to battle we went out.
How else would we have so triumphant been
And on the very first day of revolt
Exterminate three companies of SS?

55

Moshe
Yes, that was a historic day indeed,
When like one man the ghetto rose to arms.

Israel
How were they shocked, those men of the SS
When from the upper stories and the roofs
A rain of bullets poured down their heads
Until not one survived to tell the tale.
The gatherers of the ransom followed suit
And with them security police,
Of which the greater number joined our ranks.

Moshe
Perhaps they did, but they have been lukewarm
And not a single one has shown himself
To be a worthy comrade in our ranks.

Israel
It is as you have said, nevertheless
It has not hindered us in our great fight.

Moshe
The day that followed saw our flag unfurled
And the procession which had been proclaimed
In honour of the Führer was postponed
Because the circumstances were disturbed.

Israel
Then came the onslaught on the Christians
Who live in their own quarters nearby.
The Nazis trembled at the likelihood
Of our revolt developing outside.
So it went on, searches and slaughterings
And through the night the Nazis prowled about,
Their tanks a deadly music keeping up.

Moshe
When they succeeded to break down the gate
They were convinced that victory was theirs.

Were not their tanks within the ghetto walls?
But then our strategy came into play.
We closed the way against their infantry
By mounting a new post against the gate.
And in between their infantry was trapped,
While on their heads a rain of bombs came down;
No matter where they ran, they were exposed
And total victory remained with us.

Israel
Do not forget that we, too, paid in blood
For on the field we left our martyred dead.

Moshe
A hero's death was that of Samuel;
I saw him die. The fight was at its height,
And all the tanks, but one, had burst in flames.
That one, in desperation, turned to flee
When Samuel, already badly hit,
Leaped on the armoured giant, climbed aloft,
And in the turret threw a hand grenade
Which killed them all together with its blast.

Israel
A hero's death is worth two thousand lives.
The Warsaw Ghetto will remember him.

Moshe
The women are coming; let us cheer them now.

Hannah
[*Very excited*]
My husband, comrades, tell me where he is.

Moshe
I was with him up there an hour ago
And he asked me to send you his regards.

Israel

They all are in good heart and full of fire
And looking forward to renew the fray.
[*To* Esther]
And for you, Esther, have I brought regards
From Mordecai who has but now returned.
The last of all the armouries are ours
And he, together with his men, came back,
Proud and victorious. But now we, too, must go,
Our place is in the battle line again.

Moshe

Shalom Aleichem. [*Exeunt*]

Esther

Why is it, Mother, that he always seeks
Those places where the perils seem the worst?
Is danger just for him? Does he not know
That the same bullet that might strike him down,
Would strike me, too, by striking down my love?

Hannah

What are these foolish thoughts, these idle dreams?
Have you forgotten where we are, my dear?
This is no time for personal emotions,
You know your father's wish, that we should leave
Unless we hold the Nazis tyrants off.
You, who have savoured of the thrill of love
And doubtless still are vibrant with its glow,
You must be grateful for all that has passed,
But for the future, pluck out all those thoughts
So that your suffering will be the less.

Esther

Oh, Mother, help me in this darkest mood,
And comfort me before the very brink;
Sustain me with your fortitude and calm.
I dreamed of happiness in my land,
And of the flowering of our romance,
Then came the deadly storm that blighted us.

Hannah

My darling daughter, when your father comes
Conceal from him the tears in your eyes.
His burdens are already great enough
Without the further troubles that are yours.
With confidence your father faces fate,
While you, unhappily, share not his faith.

Esther

In vain, in vain are all these dreams of yours,
False hopes all those which we have worshipped here,
The tombstone is erected facing us
And wreathed in death's own blooms we see it clear.

Hannah

It is no deathly wreath that you behold,
But rather it's an all-conquering crown,
Just as each spring shoot conquering the turf,
So will our efforts be with triumph crowned.
Where you see only death and desolation
You should see life and victory portrayed.

Esther

I can look back in sadness and with tears,
Since unrequited have my passions been.
Had I, like you, gathered life's lovely flowers
Then would I, too, have been contented now.
But in our case, death blighted us so soon,
And daylight had not yet dispelled the dew
Before we were destroyed by cruel fate.
How sweet is life, why should we suffer thus?

Hannah

Wipe off those tears and do not let him see
The signs of sobbing and of violent grief.
Do not believe that our lives were so gay
And that our love was flourishing always.
For us, too, many a flower lived
But one brief moment, then died all too soon.

[Michael *enters accompanied by* Mordecai, *they are covered with dust and battle-worn*]

Michael
My dearest wife.

Hannah
May you be ever blessed.

Mordecai
Esther. Light of my life.

Esther
At last we meet.

Hannah
How did you fare? Has victory crowned your arms?

Michael
Our lives this time hung by a thread alone.
But our morale remained unconquerable.
And when our reinforcements joined us, too,
The reinforcements from the *Privileged*,
The people of the Little Ghetto here,
Although they had the chance to stay away
Six thousand of them came to swell our ranks
The flower of our youth stood by our side.

Mordecai
It was indeed a blessed victory.
After street battles we seized everyone
Of the arms stores within the ghetto walls.
There we found uniforms, which, being worn
Confused the Nazis when we struck again.
A splendid hoard of loot it was, indeed,
But at a heavy cost in men and blood.

Michael

What matters it, today or yesterday,
Or should tomorrow mark their mortal end.
They died as heroes, we should envy them.

Hannah

But how much longer can we still hold out?

Michael

No harder question have you ever asked.

Esther

But Father, tell us nothing but the truth.

Michael

Without a miracle, one month at most.

Mordecai

Where shall I find you, Esther, as we planned?

Michael

The latest word that we received
Is that SS troops will be now withdrawn
For they have made their minds up to destroy
The whole rebellion with regular troops.
And that, in brief, means war until the end,
Not guns alone, but also from the air
And if required then they will burn us out
Or by blockade to starve us in our homes.
No, no, we shall not die like that, I swear,
But rather shall we fight right to the end
And kill them so long as we have the strength.

Esther

But what of us, your daughter and your wife?

Michael

I have made plans for you, my darling ones,
And through the sewers will you find a way,
By underground you will the forest reach
And there the partisans will welcome you.
When the last battle is quite at its peak
Then you must get away on safer paths
And from outside the struggle you will wage.
The help we waited for has not arrived,
But you shall tell the world about our fight
And how your comrades all lie buried here.
Do not be nervous, everything is planned
And Mordecai himself will be your guide.

Mordecai

Nay, Michael, this one thing I shall not do.

Michael

What is this now, do you not want to save
Your fiancée and her dear mother, too?

Mordecai

I have received my training at your hands
And you have seen how proud I was to bear
My arms and how my heart swelled up with pride
When to my care your treasure you consigned,
Your only daughter, apple of your eye.
And now you ask me to disgrace myself,
To wound my soul with self-inflicted shame?
You shall not cut me off in death from those
Whose heroism I have shared hereto.
No, Father, come what may, this is too much.
I am a member of the fighting force
And where my comrades stand, there I stand, too.

Michael

Beloved son, young hero, all the same
You must do in spite of all. Look at her tears.
Through you alone she can return to life

And you alone can show her Paradise.
Yours is the privilege, yours the noble joy,
And to my daughter's heart you owe this debt.

Mordecai

Before that comes another debt for me,
A debt unto my people, not yet paid.
[*To* Esther]
My heart, my love, my feeling, and my soul,
All that is yours, and yours it will remain.
But what is it that we on earth call life?
A fragment in eternity, no more.
Each in his petty lifetime owes this debt
Toward our people's glorious heritage.
Therefore, my private feelings are suppressed
And in this ghetto fight I must remain.
In the eternal life, when next we meet
I shall be proud to greet you, knowing well
That I did not leave debts unrepaid.
So go alone, and please remember me
As one who loved you dearly but remained
And cast aside all personal desires
To serve his people when his duty called.
Why do you weep? Have I inflicted pain,
For if I have, that was not my desire.
My love for you quite equals yours for me
And makes my sacrifice no easier.
But what of that? My life has long been pledged
And to death dedicated by myself.
My life, no longer mine, I consecrate
Unto my people's cause unto the end.

Hannah

Unto this moment, I, too, had the hope
That *we* would break out of the Nazi ring
And get through safely to the partisans.
I would have been with you in full accord
To seek refuge in forests vast.

But now you have embraced your destiny
And in this ghetto to the end remain.
So be it; but your fate is mine
And life or death, my place is at your side.
My husband's fight is mine, and when you fall
The selfsame bullet will strike me down, too,
Unless at midnight comes deliverance
And sees the Allies save us as we hoped.

Michael

And what of Esther?

Hannah

She agrees with me.
Is Mordecai not the man of her choice
And death with him is much to be preferred
To life in desolation and despair?
Is she not our own child, and yet you doubt
Her answer to a problem such as this?

Esther

[Hesitating with glowing eyes]
Yes, Father, this you surely understand.
This ghetto now is taking the last stride
Toward a glorious and collective doom,
But in that doom not unaccompanied,
For just as Samson slew the Philistines
When pulling down their heathen temple walls,
So shall we, too, in fighting to the last
Take with us to the grave our bitter foes.
Can you deny me this, or even try,
When you should know how much I share the pride
Of all of you in this great final fight?
Believe me, please. I have not yet lost hope,
But rather see, in days not far removed,
The sun shine on us in our hour of joy,
And through our tears will victory's smile appear.
So be it life or death, we shall not part,
In this world and beyond, our love will live.

Mordecai

What gallant women, and how pure their hearts.
How can one stand against such steadfastness?

Michael

[*To* Mordecai]
Yet you shall go but not in hasty flight,
Rather to carry on our flaming torch
And another town in Bialystok start the revolt.
The general scheme has long since been prepared.
And you, my daughter, shall go with him, too,
My blessing will protect you on your way,
Engulfed with risks is this your honeymoon . . .
[Esther *is encouraged and embraces* Mordecai]

Mordecai

This mission willingly we undertake
But please, remember that we shall return
Since Warsaw's ghetto for us signifies
The struggle of our people to arise.

Michael

Come to me, children, for a last embrace
Come safely back to yonder place.
Whatever fate awaits us, life or death,
We shall resist them till the final breath.

End of Scene 1

SCENE 2

In the cellar of the headquarters in Nalevky Street. Abraham and Itzhak are busy cleaning machine guns. Netka is restlessly pacing up and down.

Netka
We cannot carry on like this, I say
Each night brings added terror to us here,
As endlessly the big guns thunder on,
And all the houses burn with mighty flames.

Abraham
We knew our fate full well, right from the first.
When we unfurled the banner of revolt
We knew the Nazis would, if all else failed
Bring heavy guns to wipe the ghetto out.

Itzhak
Did you imagine that our luck would hold
As once it did, when owing to the fact
That gunfire was threatening German homes
Adjacent to the battered ghetto walls
The Germans brought the barrage to an end?

Netka
Six weeks have gone since first we struck at them.
At first we were full forty thousand strong
And with our early triumphs we were sure
That we could hold out until help arrived.
I ask you, comrades, how could we believe
That all the parties of the underground
Would rush to help the ghetto in its fight?
And when we stormed the prison, and released
The prisoners, who, being political,
We deemed to be inclined to join our ranks;
We found that hopes had been betrayed
And that ingratitude was our reward.

Abraham

It is quite true that we have been deceived
But at the same time we must not forget
That side by side with us, in those dark days
The Socialist Guard fought on, and gave us help.

Itzhak

Do you remember, when they stormed our walls,
The Germans laughed to see our houses burn
And then the Socialist Guards enraged, like us,
Shot down their gunners and silenced the guns?

Abraham

They guarded every manhole in the town
And stood as sentinels by open drains
Through which escaped great numbers to the woods
To join the partisans and still fight on.

Netka

That is the point round which my thoughts revolve.
It was so futile to revolt from here,
And we should rather have made up our minds
To leave the ghetto and fight from outside.

Abraham

The fact that matters is that here we fought
And if we fall, our monument will be
The ruins all around us in this place.

Netka

No, not for me is such a monument,
I fought for life, for vengeance, and for hope,
And not for martyrdom or history.
I call to mind the glorious early days,
When our fresh hatred thrived in ruthless fight
And we saw evidence of victory.
Not empty words of glamour or of fame.
I shall not stay in Warsaw any more,
And go to break the cordon and escape.
[*Runs out*]

Abraham
Netka, be careful, wherefore are you bound?

Itzhak
There is no point in calling, she is gone;
Her mind has been made up since long.

Abraham
Who is to say that she is not quite right,
But let us not leave Michael all alone,
For he is quite determined to remain.
Did not he swear, to the last drop of blood?

Itzhak
How shall we tell him that Netka has gone?

Abraham
I see him now, and clouded with deep thoughts
Mordecai and his daughter are not back
And not a word of news from Bialystok.

Itzhak
[*Sunk in thoughts*]
She meant so much to him; he understood
Her every mood and every turn of thought.
Tell me, Abraham, did you not seem to see
A festive look on Michael's face today,
A look of triumph shining in his eyes,
As though the thought of facing foe once more
Were tonic for him and a stimulant?
I, too, had this same feeling when we slew
The Nazis in the first days of revolt.

Abraham
That is but nervousness that goes with youth
And is not part of heroism's blend.
If so, indeed, you saw his face today.
There is some other reason, not the fight.
I think that he prepares himself for death

In this last battle for his people's cause.
You will soon know if my views are the right,
For here he comes.

Itzhak

I will agree with you.

[Michael *enters by a concealed door*]

Michael

Has Mordecai not yet returned, my friends?
But yet I have no doubt that he will come
Before the last house in the ghetto falls
The final hours swiftly drawing nigh.
One death squad has been finally dispersed,
The squad that earned such glorious renown
And stood victorious at Okopowa,
Has failed to break the cordon and get out.
[Abraham *and* Itzhak *look at each other, fearful of the fate of* Netka]
I make my last appeal to all our men
And come what may, firm hearts shall we display.
I only ask for speed, my brethren, haste.

Abraham

We are all ready and will come at once.
[*Goes out with* Itzhak]

Michael

Here stand I at Death's threshold, at the last.
Tomorrow brings oblivion and night.
This is the climax of my life's desires
And this the moment when I search my soul.
I know full well that not in vain we fought
And our great efforts will not go for naught.
And if in struggle our own lives are lost,
Almighty God will balance out the cost.
This century will fade away in time
And those who knew us will all pass away.
But we, I feel, will not forgotten be,
And Jews will think of us with gratitude

So that our memory will never fade.
Even in youth I seemed to be prepared
For some great struggle at some future date
And into battle joyfully I rushed
Aware of this my rendezvous with Fate.
Now comes the final journey, and I feel
That I shall earn the finest crown of all,
When fighting for my own tormented race
My end shall come as on the field I fall.
Our poets have not lacked heroic deeds
As inspiration for their eager pen,
And now Bar Kochba and the Maccabees
Shall find their modern counterparts again.
Fate can decree the end of mortal span,
But every soul finds refuge in the skies
And earthward comes, to swell my people's ranks
By being born again in other guise.
[Hannah *enters carrying a lantern*]

Michael
How quiet you are, my wife, why is it so?

Hannah
I have prepared myself for what may come
And wait with patience for deliverance.

Michael

[*Embracing her*]

This is the way to face our last embrace,
With mutual love and hearts that beat as one.
My dearest wife, this is the time for me
To thank you for the happiness you brought,
And for the blessings I derived from you.
How constant have you been, since first we wed,
How loyal to me when trouble came our way,
Sharing my burdens, lessening my woes.
For all this, dearest wife, will you be blessed
And in the coming world earn your reward.

70

Hannah

Oh, Husband mine and hero that you are,
All that I did was in humility,
In love, and in respect for you alone.
Because of this, it was my only aim
To stay with you unto the very end.

Michael

Esther and Mordecai have not come back,
Therefore, you grieve, and yet within my heart
I hear a voice that says, "They will return."
Come to me, wife, our friends are coming back,
Let me announce our triumph over death.
[Abraham, Itzhak, Joesph, Malka, Moshe *and* Israel *enter with scores
of the Jewish Fighters' Organisation still surviving in the ghetto. They
stand in a semicircle round* Michael. Hannah *slips away slowly, holding
the candlestick in her hands, while* Michael *begins his address.*]

Abraham

All but the sentries stationed on the roof
We are assembled here at your command.

Michael

Ah well, my brethren, this must mark the end
And this will be my last address to you.
Firstly, I must give all of you due praise
For your great efforts and your loyalty,
And with a joyful heart I thank you all.
No traitors have existed in your ranks,
None shirked and none have yielded to despair.
The oath we swore, by all has been fulfilled.
This fight has been for us a victory
And all who made the supreme sacrifice
Have contributed to our people's cause.
Yes, friends of mine, you may indeed be proud,
For in this fight we rose to splendid heights
And future generations will retell
In legendary form, our matchless deeds.
Those who have fallen have not died in vain
And in their death they are with victory crowned.

71

Now death has trapped us all; there is no way
To keep at bay our foes' superior might.
Yet not for nothing have our comrades died
And thousands of the Nazis have died, too.
From underground our strongholds have been mined
And from the air bombarded endlessly,
No wall remains erect, no house still stands,
Except this one from which our flag still flies.
The Polish Underground has paid no heed
To our appeals to join in the revolt.
Our voices went unheard, lost in the wind,
While they went on debating what to do.
[*The last line is spoken in bitter irony*]
Yet we should greet Death's coming with a hymn,
Not that we did not, all of us, love life,
And for our people, wanted to live on,
But fate had other plans, as now we know.
Dastards had slaughtered millions of our brethren
But now their honour fully avenged.
Shall we now weaken from our great resolve
And die of mere starvation after all?
No, friends of mine, we'll seek a warrior's end,
One which our ancestors would not decry
And one befitting those Jews yet unborn.
We will not fall except in mortal fight
Surrounded by the corpses of the foe.
Then each one who so dies fulfils his oath
And immortality shall claim his name.

All

For the last fight the ghetto stands prepared.

[*To* Moshe]   **Michael**
What, tears in your eyes?

Moshe

But tears of joy, they are.
Joy to face death with comrades such as these,
No finer prize could any man desire.
[Mordecai *enters breathless, with* Esther, *pistol in hand.*]

Mordecai

Hello, my friends, my father. What is this?
[*Embracing him*]

Michael

I knew the final fight would see you here.

[*Embracing her father*]   ## Esther

My dearest Father. Where is Mother now?

Michael

Doubtless she is upstairs and at her post.
[*While he is hugging his daughter and stroking her face and hair, a strong
exchange of firing is heard. He leaves* Esther *at once*]

Michael

Outside, my brothers, to our final fight.

All

To take revenge and vindicate our race.

[Michael *and the others run out. Only* Mordecai *and* Esther *remain
in the cellar. The firing continues.*]

Mordecai

One more kiss and then we, too, must part.

Esther

No, no. Is this how you would want to go?
Amid this storm take your last leave of me?
Do you imagine that I should implore
The bestial Nazis to grant death's release?

Would you prefer that I die at their hands
And this flesh of mine, which is all yours,
Which thrilled for you and yearned for your caress;
Think you that I shall wait for such a death?
No, Mordecai, your bullet shall me slay
And your last kiss shall be the kiss of death.

Mordecai
What are you asking for, sweet darling mine?

Esther
'Tis good that I still have the strength for this
For otherwise I might have tried to flee
When brought before the gallows by those beasts.
Now fear I nothing and myself will press
The trigger and will find death's own release.

Mordecai
How could I kill you? That I could not do.
Already have I been so close to death.
My brother at my side was stricken down,
And o'er my parents' corpses I declared
That I would sow the seeds of death among
Our enemies so long as I had breath.
With mines packed in my case, I walked about
And nothing feared and felt no trace of nerves,
For me the enemy was just a life
That had to be extinguished by my hand.
But here to crush this gentle, tender rose?
When a mighty oak falls in a storm
And crashes to the ground amid its peers,
It does not harm the gentle grass beneath . . .
So shall it be with me, for I may fall
But not to harm thee is my destiny.
No, no, Esther, this thing I cannot do.

Esther

If you indeed have borne true love for me
And love me yet, despite this raging storm,
If you still hold our love in high esteem
And value faith and freedom and the right.
Then kill me for I know beyond all doubt
That in the world to come we shall be joined.
Do not refuse me if indeed you love.
In any case death waits; if you refuse
The Nazis will despoil me ere I die
And I will sink far lower than the grave.

Mordecai

Oh, stop, Esther, I will do as you say.
[*He draws his pistol and wants to fire*]

Esther

Not this way shall you shoot, but quietly.
You shall discharge the pistol at my heart.
Embrace me now. Ah, fortunate am I.
All seems so clear and vivid for me now
And all the mists have faded from my eyes
And in my soul there glows a magic dawn.
Yes, kill me as you kiss me this last time
So that my life departs in your embrace.

Mordecai

Do you imagine that in afterlife
We shall find happiness and rest from strife?

Esther

My dearest love, we shall together live
And taste the joys that only Heav'n can give.

Mordecai

Will you still search for me in realms sublime?

Esther

You know my love for you shall outlive time.

Mordecai
And if the battle calls, what then, dear heart?

Esther
When duty calls, you know that we must part,
And if you succumb to Death's icy hand
I shall await you on the Heavenly strand.

Mordecai
Seek in this kiss God's blessing, Esther dear.
[*He kisses her and fires a shot. She falls to the earth*]

Esther
Thank you, my darling, for so sweet a death,
Now I am spared the Nazi house of shame.
They will not number me as one more prize.
And do not keep me waiting long for you.
One final kiss to speed my soul away.
[*She dies*]

Mordecai
Rest in peace, sweet fiancée of mine.
[*Outside the sound of firing and explosions increases*]
Listen, my comrades call me to the fray.
I come, my comrades, to fight at your side.
[*He places the body of* Esther *near the back wall*]
A cellar shall be her last resting place.
And now I go upstairs, to war's black roar,
To play my part and then join you in death.
[*He wants to run out but a volley of bullets stops him. He fires back with both his pistols*]
Ha, scoundrels, I shall force you to retreat.
[*He runs to the second secret exit, but suddenly a grenade is thrown into the corridor.* Mordecai *jumps backwards. Outside the shooting continues*]
To Hell with them. The house is in their hands
But I still hear our pistols firing back.
The staircase is in their hands, too, I fear.
This is the end, there is no other way.

[*He suddenly has an idea. Stopping, he lifts the revolver*]
Ha! Enemies of my people, I escape.
One bullet still remains to set me free.
I come to join you, Esther, darling mine.
[*He goes over to the corpse and shoots himself in the head*]
Heart of my heart, my debt in blood is paid,
Betrothed mine, I come, be not dismayed.
[*He dies*]

Martial music continues as Scene 2 ends

SCENE 3

Evening and twilight. A heavy fight is going on before the headquarters in Nalevky Street. The last attack—a party of Nazis is coming from behind.

Nazi Officers
[*Shouting in the direction of the upper stories.*]
Cease fire, rebels, fighting is in vain.
You are the only ones who still remain.
Throw down your arms and you can all go free
But if you fight, no mercy will there be.

Abraham
[*Revealing himself from a window on the top floor*]
You waste your time, and you may save your breath,
Your unclean mouths should only speak of death,
A new race has arisen and defies
Those cruel tyrants, cursed from the skies.
You who have killed, yourselves shall now be slain
And you who tortured shall yourselves bear pain.

He throws a handgrenade at them. The fight begins again. Gradually it becomes dark. The voice of the Nazi is heard saying, "Set fire to the house." Suddenly the building is in flames. The last ghetto rebels, Michael, Abraham, and Isaac, appear on the roof, wrapped in their national colours. The last defenders seek a hero's death rather than fall into the hands of the scourge of Israel. Finally, no alternative remaining, they leap into the flames . . . the Nazi party advances. A song of mourning rises and falls—the three bodies of the leaders of the revolt are shrouded in the flags. They lie on the ground between the falling walls.

[*Hannah enters, holding a lamp, stops in horror before the bodies, and lifts the flags slightly. Her weeping reveals her deep anguish*]

Hannah
They all lie there, death has claimed them now.
Heroes they were, defiant to the end.

Be ye at peace, ye champions of our race.
My friends, my husband, rest in peace at last
While my mind wanders over the last scenes . . .
The rising and the splendour of those days,
The great high hopes, the thrill of fighting back
When honour came back to the ghetto walls
And made us conscious of our dubious fate.
Nights without slumber, days of constant toil,
Forever striving to attain the aim
Of liberating your community.
Yet those who were your charges paid no heed;
They closed their eyes and turned to you deaf ears.
Now you are gone, torn from my very heart
And, dead with you, are your secrets, but to me
They shall remain quite unforgettable.
My family gone, how bitter is my fate!
My daughter and my son-in-law lie dead
And here the light of my life is extinct.
[*She breaks into tears*]
Why should I weep and give way to these tears?
Should I, above all others, not perceive
That millions have been overwhelmed like this
And that the Jewish people mourning sits
In sorrow for the ghastly sacrifice,
Attired in sacks and ashes on their heads,
Praying by candles lit in memory.
Jews in the future shall with grief recall
This deadly nightmare that engulfed us all,
This tyrant with his crooked swastika
Whose doom is prayed for by all who survive.
Will not the dead emerge from out their graves
Their faces darkened by their sufferings,
Decayed and trembling, but accusing still?
Can these forgotten be, hunted and slain
In every land where Jews had lived before?
They dared to rise and strike back at the foe
Seeking revenge, determined to resist
Rather than suffer in a living hell
Accepting meekly all the blows of fate.

For them the death was Samson's, death with pride,
The death of heroes who have known no fear.

[*She caresses the body of* Michael. *As her fingers touch his chest she finds a note case in his inner pocket*]

How could I not remember? In this case
You often told me you had left your will,
The testament of all who fought with you.
What did he mean, I wonder, by those words?

[*With trembling hands she brings out a paper card, and begins to read, but first looks round as if afraid of being surprised*]

"If we should fall in this last bloody fight
And leave our hopes for ever unfulfilled,
Then bring to mind the legend of old Greece.
Prometheus had brought down from Heaven, fire
And found himself condemned to punishment
For being guilty of so great a crime.
Chained to a rock, food for the vultures' greed
He resolutely all the pain endured,
And only asked: 'The fire, does it burn?'
Thus shall you hear, though we are long since gone,
The echo of our voices, crying yet
'The fire we lit, does it still burn for us?'
The fire we kindled in the ghetto walls
While vainly we awaited the Messiah.
Our call to arms still rings out in the air
And after twenty centuries we rose
For honour fighting and for liberty."

[Hannah *looks as in a dream at the piece of paper in her hands. Suddenly she springs to life. Steps are heard from both sides and bullets whistle through the air. From one side, two SS men enter and fall. One of them in falling fires at* Hannah *who falls across the body of her husband. From the other side* Netka *enters with two young men armed with pistols and guns. She tries, helped by one of the men, to lift* Hannah. *The other young man searches both sides. He examines the fallen Nazis and takes their weapons.*]

80

Netka

Oh, Hannah, have you fallen to the foe?
Rally your strength and come with us. We go.
Your wounds will heal and you will still remain
To join the underground and fight again.

Hannah

[*With her last strength*]
No, Netka, you must go, wait not for me.
Do you not see on whom I now repose?
'Neath me the bodies of our leaders lie,
And with my husband I shall here remain.
Even if I agreed, it is too late;
You must go on and leave me to my fate.
Only remember to tell all the world
How here the Jewish flag was first unfurled.

[Hannah *gives her the case and card and falls back.* Netka *kisses her and the flag covering* Michael, *and sadly goes off with the two men. The lamp fades. A dirge is heard in the distance.* Hannah *arouses herself for the last time*]

God of Israel, with my failing breath,
Hear my last prayer going to my death.
Grant us that our fight was not in vain
And that our nation will rise up again.
That all our sufferings shall pass away
And leave us, to enjoy a brighter day,
A day of peace and plenty, joy and calm,
No longer haunted by the foe's alarm.
Shine on us, then, and bathe us in your rays
And grant your children happiness always.

[*She falls back and dies. Darkness. Gradually the final music swells up with chords of hope, giving promise, at the moment of her death, of the full redemption of Jewry.*]

End of Act III

Epilogue

Long praise the hymn the valiant rebels
Who rang in their falls yet the freedom bells;
Blessed is their vengeance and holy their hatred;
A legend of fame they forever created.

In the flow of the times how inflicted the fate
Blows of distress on my brethren in hate.
All over the globe like drops of the dew
Sprinkle the wormwood-tears of the Jew.

Oh, tears of revolt, of sorrow and grief
For the dearest on earth our foes did bereave;
Loud clamors the glow, and a flame in the breath
Whispers a prayer: Revenge for their death!

Oh, Europe, thy soil's penetrated of blood,
Of the red-glutted streams that flooded thy mud,
From innocent victims, from martyrs pure,
From the sons of my nation who fought to endure.

The cry of thy roots filled with blood and with tears
Uprises to heaven, jars on my ears . . .
Is driven aloft like a breeze by a jolt
And bursts through thy clods to call for revolt.

All cruelty acts were perceived on thy soils,
All murders and tortures, all torments and toils . . .
The blood-swollen flesh in the deepness lay
To thunder as witness on Judgement Day!

The horror-proof in the millions of bullets
Strewn from machine-guns and pistol gullets;
They sank into earth, in the bodies the lead,
Yet their tinge is so red from the blood that was shed.

No border confines there the graveyard, immense—
From Majdanek to Savidor it extends;
To Auschwitz and Treblinka hastened the trains
In terror satiated, replenished with pains.

The death-waggons rushed. No power did stop
Israel's sons rode their mortal gallop
Like sheep to their stable, and not to the pyre,
To the chambers of gas or to vapours of fire. . . .

At night, in my dreams, the shadows appear,
Stricken by lashes, starvation, and fear,
The symbol of pangs, despair, and all evil:
Crushed are the bones, in affliction of devil.

Unto the day when the ghetto uprose
And the conscience defending honour chose.
With sparks in their eyes and arms in the fist,
The ghetto stood up the foe to resist.

Each building befitted a fortress in field,
Each cellar and sewer like David's shield.
The fighters erected at last barricades
Abjured alleged cowardice for all decades.

With machine-guns, revolvers, yet heavily shelled,
Against legions of Nazis the ghetto rebelled.
Till tanks, heavy cannons and planes intervened . . .
The ghetto was conquered—wrecked and ruined.

Yet the flame of rebellion never did fade
In the vow like steel for posterity made.
It's a will to withstand, toward freedom to strive,
To guard like Cherubs at the Arbor of Life!

No king gave those fighters a medal of merit,
Unknown are the heroes whose laud we inherit.
Their brethren who proudly were lifted from bale
Shall honour the deeds for beloved Israel.

Long praise the hymn the valiant rebels
Who rang in their fall yet the freedom bells.
Blessed is their vengeance and sacred their story,
Eternal their flame and immortal their glory!

About the Author

Harry Shadmon was born in Vienna between the two world wars as son of a well-known Russian physician and a Czechoslovakian mother. As a youngster he succeeded in escaping Nazi Europe to Palestine, where he was active during the pre-state years in the underground. In the Israeli army he commanded POW camps and later, in the reserves, he was a liaison officer with UNTSO, the United Nations Truce Supervision Organisation, in the Golan Heights. A trained economist and an accomplished linguist in several European and Mid East languages, he wrote the epos of *Ghetto Rebels* in its original Hebrew version soon after World War II, when the events of those days stirred his and the souls of millions of others.